C000045784

Thank you, Nolma & A
for your care and attention.
to me.
from, Jerry attrick.

The
Lake District
is a Garden

The Lake District is a Garden

A wayfarer's companion

Catherine Hamilton

Select Editions

in association with
David Bateman

Dedication

For Jacquie

Acknowledgements

I am deeply grateful to many people who, by their kindness, friendship, and willingness to share their great love of flowers and historical heritage, made the work for this book not only possible but an event of great joy.

My special thanks to Anne Barnes, Gladys and Michael Beattie, Roger and Nick Burley, K.F. Brown, H. Catling, George Kirkby, Lord and Lady Tranmire, Mary and the late Tom Cook, Alan Newton, Dr and Mrs Delap, Miss E. Webb, Jacquie Spiers, Frances Lonsbrough, Jean Spiceley, and Janette and Bill Chynoweth and family.

A very special thank you to my sister and travelling companion, Bernadette Spiers, for her patient, enthusiastic assistance, to the late Ruth and Bob Hamilton, and Eileen and Lew Fell who looked after my children whilst I was away on my journey; and finally, David Bateman, for his continued confidence in my ability.

First published in 1993 in Great Britain by
Bracken Books, a division of Studio Editions Ltd
in association with David Bateman Ltd

This edition published by Select Editions,
Selectabook Distribution Centre,
Folly Road, Roundway, Devizes,
Wiltshire SN10 2HR

ISBN 1-85891-033-1

Printed and bound in India

Design by David Bateman Ltd

Contents

Introduction

"Rent a caravan, wander around, paint and sketch anything that catches your eye" was my publisher's brief, on this occasion, for my visit to the Lake District. To experience the romantic charm of the area was a unique and wonderful experience. I wandered at will, recording in pencil and watercolour, the magic of the scenery, the buildings steeped in history, and the gentle beauty of wild and cultivated flowers and trees. I revelled in the wealth of literary association, local character and tradition, of this "Magnificent Jewel in England's crown" which attracts and delights vast numbers of tourists throughout the summer months.

It is hard for any visitor to the Lake District area to record even a small proportion of the impressions gathered on a journey such as this — the first light of day, filtering through a gentle mist and touching the peaceful water of a tranquil lake; families of "Beatrix Potter" bunnies out to play before the sound of man and vehicles send them scurrying away; tiny squirrels frolicking under tall trees; lakeside and fell walks. All these are precious memories but it was the glorious flowers and magnificent trees that were the most spectacular and beautiful attraction for me.

I shall always remember fondly the willingness of local folk to invite me to share their gardens — from impressive historic houses with walled gardens, to tiny cottage gardens, their knowledge of local flora, and their concern that this heritage should be protected.

I hope this book will enable you to share some of my experiences and help you to remember some of this natural and man made beauty.

The Lake District has been home for many writers, including Beatrix Potter whose tales of Peter Rabbit, Jemima Puddleduck and many other creatures continue to enchant me. They were successful right from the beginning, and in 1905 Beatrix Potter bought Hill Top Farm, which I *had* to sketch. Subsequently she bought several other properties in the area and bequeathed many to the National Trust. She died in 1944 at the age of 78.

Hill Top Farm, near Sawry, home of Beatrix Potter
Pump at Hill Top Farm

PANSIES
THE PROVENCE ROSE (*Rosa centifolia*)

The river Dee winds through Lower
Dentdale and provides a very beautiful way
to either enter or leave the Lake District

Lower Dentdale

COWSLIP (*Primula veris*)

Although thought to be 13th century, the exact origin of the bridge at Kirkby Lonsdale is unknown; legend claims it was built overnight by the Devil! There are some beautiful walks in the area and John Ruskin, the 19th century art critic and social reformer, said the view from the town was "one of the loveliest in England—therefore in the world".

I spotted there one of my favourite butterflies.

The Devil's Bridge, Kirkby Lonsdale

SPEAR THISTLE (*Cirsium vulgare*)
PAINTED LADY BUTTERFLY (*Cynthia cardui*)

Personally, I prefer to see trees growing naturally, but I must confess the topiary at Levens Hall intrigued me! Set in 100 acres of parkland laid out in the late 17th century and unchanged since that time, the box, holly and yew trees are clipped between mid-September and Christmas each year. The hall is Elizabethan and contains many fine works of art collected during its long history, including 17th-century ornate leather hangings.

Levens Hall, near Kendal

BOX TREE (*Buxus sempervirens*)

At Cartmel I found a most unusual church built diagonally out from the tower. Originally an Augustine Priory established in the 12th century, all that is left of the original building is a gatehouse.

It is a pretty place near wooded country and close to Morecambe Bay.

Cartmel Priory Church, Cartmel

WILD CHERRY (*Prunus avium*)

I can never resist an ancient family stronghold so I was captivated by Sizergh Castle with its massive peel tower built in 1340 to defend the Strickland family from Scottish raiders; also the Tudor Great Hall and the beautiful park and gardens. The family have lived there for over 700 years, although it is now cared for by the National Trust.

Sizergh Castle, near Kendal

IVY or BOSTON IVY (*Parthenocissus tricuspidata*)

Kendal Castle
Catherine Parr's prayer book

DAMASK ROSE (*Rosa damascena*)

The Norman Kendal Castle is interesting because it was the home of Catherine Parr, the sixth and last wife of Henry VIII. Her beautifully scripted prayer book is preserved in Kendal Town Hall. In 1571 after the death of Catherine's brother, who left no heirs, the Castle was abandoned and today is a rather sombre ruin.

The town was one of the centres of the early Flemish woollen industry, hence its motto *Pannus mihi panis* (Wool is my bread). It has narrow streets winding to the river, grey stone buildings, and is full of interest.

A very special breed of sheep has helped over many centuries to successfully develop the Lakeland wool trade. The origin of the Herdwick sheep breed is obscure, though it may have come from Scandinavia. In the 12th century the monks of Furness Abbey recorded their flocks of *herdwykes*. It is an extremely hardy breed and survives the harsh mountain conditions living all year at heights up to 2000 feet and lambing there too. Their wool is long, strong and ideal for carpets and hardwearing tweeds.

Herdwick sheep, Shap Fell
Lakeland shepherds' crooks

YELLOW MOUNTAIN SAXIFRAGE (*Saxifraga aizoides*)

I love curiosities. On Belle Isle, Windermere, is a unique round house built in 1774 on the site of a Roman villa. At the time it was thought to be in bad taste and Wordsworth called it a "pepper pot". Anyway I enjoyed sketching it and the beautiful grounds.

Opposite the house is Bowness-on-Windermere, a centre for water sports. The lake is the largest in England and has been an important waterway for two thousand years at least, certainly since the Romans established the fort of Galava at the north end.

Belle Isle, Windermere
Bowness-on-Windermere

DAHLIAS

A large number of lakeland hill farms are protected by the National Trust and Yew Tree Farm is a particularly fine example. Probably originally constructed of timber, sometime during the 17th and 18th centuries it was rebuilt in stone when many farmers became involved in the wool industry. The open spinning gallery is typical of that used by spinners to get maximum daylight for their work.

It is said the farm was named after a 700-year-old yew tree which blew down in 1896. Yews are known for their extreme longevity, perhaps up to 3000 years. The wood was used for making the famous English longbow.

Yew Tree Farm, Coniston

YEW TREE (*Taxus baccata*)

Unlike that found in many great family mansions and castles, much of the furniture and panelling at Town End, a successful yeoman farmer's family home, was carved and constructed by members of the Browne family who lived there from 1623 for some 300 years. Although now owned by the National Trust and open to the public, the place exudes family atmosphere, and the initials carved into the various household items by family members who helped construct them, conjure up visions of the generations who lived and died there.

Town End, Troutbeck

HOUSE SPARROW
FOXGLOVE (*Digitalis purpurea*)

The poet William Wordsworth attended Hawkshead Grammer School around 1780. Established in the 16th century, it has not been used as a school since 1909.

Hawkshead Grammar School

NASTURTIUM (*Tropaeolum minus*)

Wordsworth lodged in this cottage while he attended Hawkshead Grammar school. It is typical of many others in the narrow lanes of the village.

Anne Tyson's Cottage, Hawkshead

NARCISSUS

A tarn is a small, elevated mountain lake as opposed to the larger lakes or "waters" in the valleys. There are several hundred in the Lake District. The highest is Broadcrag Tarn at 2750 feet. The most popular is Tarn Hows close to Coniston. Ironically, it is manmade, having been created at the end of the last century by damming the outlet from three swampy tarns to form a large, irregularly shaped single tarn with two small islands. It is now a very beautiful spot with plantations of larch, spruce and pine, surrounded by rolling fells reaching for the sky.

Tarn Hows, near Coniston

LILY

Brantwood, the home of John Ruskin, is well worth a visit. A delapidated 18th-century cottage when he bought it, he renovated and extended it over the years to make a very comfortable home. Today, it still contains a large collection of his furniture, his own watercolours, other works of art and personal possessions. It also has magnificent views across Coniston Water to the mountain called The Old Man of Coniston, and of the fells around it.

Brantwood, Coniston Water

MARGUERITE DAISY (*Chrysanthemum leucanthemum*)

Built as a summer house, this quaint 17th-century rough-stone structure "Bridge House" is now a tourist information centre. Surely the nursery rhyme, *The Old Woman who lived in a Shoe* was written with this little house in mind? Be that true or not, I was told that a woman with a very large family did, indeed, live there once upon a time . . .

On a walk to Stockghyll Force Waterfall nearby, I found this native balsam or touch-me-not, and white clover in full bloom.

Bridge House, Ambleside

TOUCH-ME-NOT (*Impatiens nolitangere*)
WHITE CLOVER (*Trifolium repens*)

Rydal Water is a delightful small lake lying between Grasmere and Windermere. Closeby is the charming, 16th century house, Rydal Mount, where Wordsworth lived from 1813 till his death in 1850. Whilst I was quietly painting the lake I chanced to see this woodpecker.

Rydal Water

GREAT SPOTTED WOODPECKER (*Dendrocopos major*)

From 1799 to 1807 Wordsworth lived at Dove Cottage. It
is much the same today as it was then. Poppies decorated
the garden wall and the wild strawberries from the garden
were delicious!

It was originally an inn called *The Dove and Olive Bough*
and Wordsworth, with his sister Dorothy, his wife and
three of his five children, spent eight of the happiest years
of his life there. He wrote of it:

Where once the Dove and Olive-Bough,
Offered a greeting of good ale,
To all who entered Grasmere Vale;
and called on him who must depart,
To leave it with a jovial heart;
There, where the Dove and Olive-Bough
once hung, a poet harbours now,
A simple, water-drinking bard . . .
       Wordsworth, *The Waggoner* 1806

Dove Cottage, Grasmere

WELSH POPPY (*Meconopsis cambrica*)
WILD STRAWBERRY (*Fragaria vesca*)

One day I strayed a little west of the main lakes to roam through lakeless Eskdale. Amongst its rocky crags and woody slopes are the sites of many ancient copper and iron mines, now abandoned. Close to the attractive village of Boot, with its old "pack horse" bridge, I painted the Eskdale corn mill. There has been a mill here since the 13th century, though the present building dates from the 16th and has been restored by the Cumbria County Council.

Eskdale Corn Mill, Boot

MARSH MARIGOLD (*Caltha palustris*)
WALL BROWN BUTTERFLY (*Lasiommata megera*)

Not far from Boot is Ravenglass. On the coast, it has a
natural harbour which was used by the Romans for 300
years. There is not much left of the fort they built but
nearby are substantial remains of their bath house. Ninety
feet long and 30 feet wide there is evidence that it
provided hot saunas and cold baths. I was told it is the best
preserved Roman building in the north of England.

There were plenty of brambles growing, as there
probably were in the days of the Romans, who used
blackberries to cure gout. Herbalists today use it to relieve
tonsillitis and sore throats. Natural dyes from the plant
produce orange from the root, soft black from young shoots
and greyish blue colours from the ripe berries. Blossom of
all kinds is beautiful but specially lovely to me was this
blackberry — its dark green foliage and delicate white
petals tinged with pink, rambling wild and free.

Roman Bath House, Ravenglass

BRAMBLE (*Rubus fruticosus*)

I never tired of my Lakeland rambles for it seemed there was always something new to see, either beautiful or curious. The Bowder Stone certainly falls into the latter category. Appearing to be delicately balanced on one edge, its huge bulk—36 feet high and 60 feet long—is actually very stable. It must be for it's been where it was deposited by a receding glacier for at least 10,000 years. Wooden steps lead to its top from where there are fine views down the valley of the River Derwent.

The Stone rests on the birch-wooded slopes of Grange Dell. In other parts of the valley, where the soil is richer, oak, beach and alder grow.

Grange Fell, Borrowdale
Bowder Stone, Borrowdale

There are many single arch, "pack-horse" bridges like Ashness Bridge. Probably built at the beginning of the 18th century and even earlier, they were a vital part of the primitive links between the isolated communities of those days. Wordsworth wrote that they were "in themselves models of elegance, as if they had been formed upon principles of the most thoughtful architecture".

I had intended to paint the leaves of the ash growing in Ashness Woods but the fuzzy "beechmast" nuts of the magnificent beech trees attracted me more.

Ashness Bridge, Borrowdale

BEECH (*Fagus sylvatica*)

This part of the Lake District is surely one of the most spectacular in England, with its towering crags and soft green, golden brown, bracken-covered lower slopes, reflected in the beautiful, tranquil lakes below.

Crummock Water

BRACKEN (*Pteridium aquilinum*)

Crummock Water is linked by a river
cascading down the spectacular fall of Scale
Force to Buttermere which I think is the
most beautiful lake of all. I walked the three
and a half miles round it, through pine
plantations and green pastures, in constant
wonder at the magnificent views. The lake
is dominated by the soaring Honister Crag
from which green slate has been mined
since the mid-1600s.

Honister Crag
Buttermere

SCOTS PINE (*Pinus sylvestris*)

One of the remotest villages I visited was Watendlath. It had no electricity until 1978 and no telephones until 1984! I walked there, along a footpath which followed the Watendlath Beck, and entered the hamlet across a sturdy "pack horse" bridge. On the way I saw many wild flowers. Sir Hugh Walpole used Watendlath as a setting in his *Herries* novels.

Watendlath, Borrowdale

FIELD POPPY (*Papaver rhoeas*)
GLOBE FLOWER (*Trollius europaeus*)
OX-EYE DAISY (*Heliopsis vulgare*)

41

For 300 years, from Elizabethan times, the fells
around Newlands Valley, west of Derwent
Water, were busy with miners digging mostly
for copper and lead ore. Then, the valley was a
centre for the metal industry. Now, it's a green
and tranquil place of fine pastures. Above
Little Town there is a tiny whitewashed
church, often the starting point for tramping
among the surrounding high fells.

Newlands Valley
Newlands Church above Little Town

BILBERRY (*Vaccinium myrtillus*)

Poet Samuel Taylor Coleridge (*The Ancient Mariner*) sometimes worked closely with Wordsworth. He wrote of Thirlmere in 1803 "let me somehow or other celebrate the world in your mirror. . : ." At that time there were two small lakes but towards the end of the century the whole valley was flooded to form a reservoir for Manchester. It is now flanked by Forestry Commission plantations which include stands of the stately Douglas fir.

Fisercraig Plantation, Thirlmere

DOUGLAS FIR

Although John Ruskin died at Coniston in 1900, there is a stone dedicated to his memory at Friars Crag, Derwent Water.

   I thought it made a lovely scene to paint and I was also interested to discover that this is one of the few woodland areas of Britain in which the Red Squirrel has survived.

Friars Crag. Derwent Water

RED SQUIRREL

I think probably the most beautiful garden I visited was Lingholm on the western shore of Derwent Water. There are formal plantings of daffodils, magnificent rhododendrons and azaleas, as well as charming mixed woodland flowers. Beatrix Potter was a frequent visitor and wrote Squirrel Nutkin here.

Lingholm, Derwent Water
Lingholm Island, Derwent Water

DAFFODILS
RHODODENDRON (*hybrid*)

47

For over 300 years botanists and taxonomists have debated the correct name for the little blue flower that carpets the English woodland glades just as the trees break into leaf. The bluebell, also known as the English Hyacinth, has had many curious popular names, including griggles, jacinth, cuckoo's boots and crowtoes.

Today the name Endymion (the woodland lover of the huntress Diana) is recommended in the Royal Horticultural Society dictionary supplement but learned debate on a flower's origin is not for me. I have simply painted a bluebell-tinted glade.

Woodland scene

ENGLISH BLUEBELLS (*Endymion nonscriptus*)

49

In 1770, William Wordsworth was born here at Wordsworth House, his parents' 18th-century house in Cockermouth, one of the most impressive and oldest towns in west Cumbria. Saved from demolition in the late 1930s by the National Trust, the house has a comfortable atmosphere with views of the River Derwent from the walled back garden.

Wordsworth House, Cockermouth

RAGWORT (*Senecio jacobaea*)
WILD STRAWBERRY (*Fragaria vesca*)

This cottage in Matterdale is typical of many in the Lake District with its dry stonework and whitened walls. The local stone is generally extremely hard so walls were often constructed of rubble.

Stone Cottage, Matterdale

HAREBELL (*Campanula rotundifolia*)
HEATHER (*Calluna vulgaris*)

The ancient boulders of Castlerigg Stone Circle were probably put in place some 3500 years ago. Wordsworth, amongst others, believed they were a Druid Temple. They stand in open pasture over 700 feet above sea level and are surrounded by the massive bulk of the Skiddaw and Helvellyn mountain ranges. The circle, roughly 100 feet in diameter and consisting of 38 stones plus a rectangle of 10 to one side, created for me a feeling of foreboding as dark clouds scudded overhead. So I lightened the mood by painting some tiny wild flowers growing in the surrounding district.

Castlerigg Stone Circle, near Keswick

SCARLET PIMPERNEL (*Anagallis arvensis*)
MOUNTAIN PANSY (*Viola lutea*)
COMMON SPEEDWELL (*Veronica officinalis*)

53

William Wordsworth, my favourite English poet and acknowledged to be the greatest Lakeland poet, lived his eighty years close to the lakes. In his *Guide to the Lakes*, first published in 1810, he wrote of Ullswater "as being, perhaps, upon the whole, the happiest combination of beauty and grandeur which any of the Lakes affords". It was in Gowbarrow Park, on its shores, that he and his sister, Dorothy, came across the daffodils "among the mossy stones" close to the water's edge which inspired this verse:

> *I wandered lonely as a cloud*
> *That floats on high o'er vales and*
>   *hills,*
> *When all at once I saw a crowd,*
> *A host, of golden daffodils;*
> *Beside the lake, beneath the trees,*
> *Fluttering and dancing in the*
>   *breeze.*

Gowbarrow Park, Ullswater

DAFFODILS (*Narcissus pseudonarcissus*)

A MEDLEY OF LAKELAND ROSES

Now a peaceful farmhouse, the medieval peel tower of
Dacre Castle has particularly well preserved battlements,
despite its turbulent history. Built in the 14th century, it is
believed to be the place where in AD 926 Athelston, the
Saxon King of Wessex, accepted the submission of all the
kings and overlords (the Danelaw) of the North of Britain,
so becoming the first true King of England.

   I was there early one morning and watched many
rabbits scampering around.

Dacre Castle

HONEYSUCKLE (*Lonicera periclymenum*)

RABBIT (*Oryctogalus cuniculus*)

The Victorians transformed the market and mining town of Keswick into a holiday centre; the scenery is superb and there are many magnificent walks. An interesting building is Moot Hall, built in 1813; its ground floor arches were originally open for use as market stalls. It is now an information centre for the National Park.

Moot Hall, Keswick

GARDEN PANSY (*Viola wittrockiana*)

Beside the River Eamont are two closely connected stronghold sites dating back to the 1st century. Here, the Roman commander Agicola built a fort, Brocavum, the outlines of which can still be seen alongside the ruins of 12th-century Brougham Castle, begun during the reign of Henry II.

Ruins of Brougham Castle, near Penrith

CALENDULA (*Calendula officinalis*)

I spent one of my most enjoyable afternoons sitting on a lawn of soft, velvet green grass behind a walled garden at Acorn Bank, a red, sandstone manor house built in the early 1700s.

Acorn Bank, Temple Sowerby

OPIUM POPPY (*Papaver somniferum*)
ORRIS ROOT (*Iris florentina*)

Between the Pennines and the Lake District lies Penrith, for hundreds of years an important stronghold on the route between England and Scotland. It is believed that a 10th-century King of Cumbria, Owen Caesarius, held court there and is buried beneath the Giant's Grave, a monument beside the Norman church. I was there in late summer as the young acorns, still green, were beginning to ripen on the oak trees.

Giant's Grave, Penrith

OAK (*Quercus robur*)

Near Glenridding, at the southern end of
Ullswater, is Greenside Mine from which lead
and silver ore was extracted from the 17th
century until its closure in 1962. Now the
buildings are used as a centre for outdoor
pursuits and by the Youth Hostel Association. I
thought they made a quaint picture.

Greenside Mine, near Glenridding

AARON'S ROD (*Verbascum thapsus*)

In the ancient town of Appleby-in-Westmorland, stands this tall Georgian "White House" with its interesting ogee-headed windows. Hidden behind the busy main street and bordering the River Eden, is one of the most attractive and tranquil gardens I found. The lawns were ready for summer croquet; tall copper beech trees, candytuft and, amongst many other flowers, this lovely Japanese anemone, provided another link with Roman times. Dioscorides, a botanist in the time of Emperor Nero, listed it in his *Codex Vindobonensis*, now one of the rarest books in the world. The viola, or horned violet from the Pyrenees, which has also grown in English gardens for centuries, complemented the anemone's pale beauty.

The "White House", Appleby-in-Westmore

JAPANESE ANEMONE (*Anemone japonica*)
VIOLA (*Viola cornuta*)

John Peel must have been quite a man and his wife Mary quite a woman! He was only 20 when they eloped to Gretna Green; they had 13 children and he kept a pack of hounds for 55 years. The song which immortalised the most famous of all huntsmen—*Do you ken John Peel?*—was by a friend, a woollen manufacturer who produced the wool for Peel's famous coat. John died aged 78 and Mary at 82. Their grave, decorated with hunting horn motifs, is in the churchyard at Caldbeck on the northern boundary of the National Park. It is another example of the curiosities I enjoy.

John Peel's grave, Caldbeck

HOLLY (*Ilex aquifolium*)

Clustered around a bridge over the River Eden is the pretty little village of Armathwaite, with its stone cottages and a peel tower (now a private house). I was attracted by the 12th-century chapel of Christ and St Mary, restored in the 17th century after use as a cowshed.

Chapel of Christ and St Mary, Armathwaite

WHITE CLOVER (*Trifolium repens*)
COMMON DOG VIOLET (*Viola riviniana*)

As I had decided to visit Carlisle, I felt I must extend my itinerary a little to see Hadrian's Wall, which was built to protect the northernmost boundary of the Roman Empire. Banks East Turret was one of many two storey look-out posts along the wall. Work began on it in AD 122 and its 73 miles took seven years to build. It was so carefully constructed and engineered that much remains today.

Banks East Turret, Hadrian's Wall, near Brampton

BELL HEATHER (*Erica cinerea*)
HAWTHORN (*Crataegus monogyna*)

Although Carlisle is not strictly in the Lake District I thought it appropriate to finish the book with a sketch of its castle because for centuries it played a vital role in the attempt by the Scots to gain control of the north of England. William II built Carlisle Castle in 1092 on the site of an ancient camp. Mary Queen of Scots went there as a guest and became a prisoner. It had a stormy history, but the outer walls are still intact and so is the 12th-century keep, the 14th-century main gate and part of Queen Mary's Tower. So it seems to me a fitting sentinel to stand as a symbolic guard over the extreme beauty and romantic history of the Lake District.

Carlisle Castle

WOOD CRANESBILL (*Geranium sylvaticum*)
CROWBERRY (*Empetrum nigrum*)

The publishers acknowledge their indebtedness to the following books and journals which were consulted for reference.
Duerden, Norman, *The Countryside of Lakeland*, Jarrold.
Finch Stanley, *Wordsworth's Flowers*, Lunsdale Publishing Group.
AA Hand-picked Tours in Britain.
AA Illustrated Guide to Britain.
AA Treasures of Britain.
Journals of Dorothy Wordsworth, Oxford University Press.
Muir, Richard, *The English Village*, Thames & Hudson.
Waller, Cliff, *Nature Guide to the Lake District*, Usborne.
Whiteman, Robin, *The English Lakes*, Weidenfeld & Nicholson.